# TAROT

ANCIENT WISDOM FOR THE NEW AGE

# TAROT

## THE SECRETS OF THE CARDS

Esmeralda da Silva

IMM lifestyle books
Read. Learn. Do What You Love.

Text, illustrations, and photographs by IMM Lifestyle Books, an imprint of Fox Chapel Publishing, 903 Square Street, Mount Joy, PA 17552. *www.foxchapelpublishing.com*

First published in 1997 by New Holland (Publishers) Ltd



Designed and edited by
40 Castelnau
London SW13 9RU

Editorial Direction: Yvonne McFarlane
Editor: Michèle Brown
Designer: Peter Ward

ISBN 978-1-5048-0162-1

FSC
www.fsc.org
MIX
Paper | Supporting responsible forestry
FSC® C147414

Printed in China
First Printing

To learn more about the other great books from Fox Chapel Publishing, or to find a retailer near you, call toll-free at 800-457-9112 or visit us at *www.FoxChapelPublishing.com*.

We are always looking for talented authors. To submit an idea, please send a brief inquiry to acquisitions@foxchapelpublishing.com.

Or write to:
Fox Chapel Publishing
903 Square Street
Mount Joy, PA 17552

This is a gift book. It is not to encourage diagnosis and treatment of illnesses, disease or other general problems by the layman. Any application of the recommendations set our in the following pages is at the reader's discretion and sole risk.

# CONTENTS

# ACROSS THE MILLENIA

In 1781, the French writer, Court de Gebelin, fascinated by myth and legend, wrote 'It is thought that all ancient wisdom was destroyed when the Great Library at

Alexandria was burned down. This is not so. One book has been handed down and with it many secrets of the ancients. It is written on seventy-eight leaves, divided into five classes.' He was describing The Tarot. According to de Gebelin, the twenty-two cards of the Major Arcana represented the temporal and spiritual leaders of ancient Egyptian society. The other fifty-six cards were divided

into four suits, the four classes of ancient Egyptian society. The king and military carried the sword, the priesthood, the cup, farmers, the stave or baton, and those engaged in commerce, the coin.

The theories about The Tarot's Egyptian origins, remain just theories. Ettiella, one of de Gebelin's followers claimed evidence that the original Tarot had been written

on gold leaves in a temple at Memphis. Others thought that the images of the twenty-two cards of the Major Arcana were painted on the walls of a subterranean galley in the Great Pyramid at Giza. The theory was compounded by stories that The Tarot had been introduced to Europe by the gypsies, whose name was a corrupt form of 'Egyptians'. It is more likely that the cards were brought by Crusaders returning from the Holy Land in the 14th century. The cards were thought to have mystical, almost demonic, powers. Referred to as the *Gypsies' Bible* and the *Devil's Book*, at various times they were banned in France, Germany and other countries.

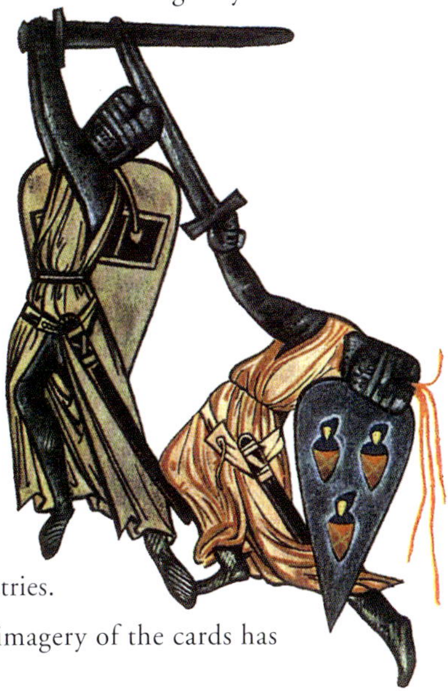

Over the years, the imagery of the cards has

remained consistent. From the 14th century some cards survive, notably the pack engraved by Mantegna, some of which are shown below. Others include those painted by Bembo for the Duke of Milan and the pack designed in 1392, by Gringonneur, for Charles the VIth of France. As new packs came into use, so the painters and interpreters absorbed the most significant imagery and momentous

events of their day, into the designs. From across the ages we now have the distilled thoughts of mystics, literally, in our hands.

The cards which illustrate the Arcana in this book are 19th-century designs from the 'Swiss' pack, *top left*, the 'Wirth' pack, *top right*, the 'Marseille' pack, *bottom left*, and the 'Rider Waite' pack, *bottom right*, which are all widely available.

# THE ARCANA

The Major Arcana, or Greater Secrets, is made up of twenty-two picture cards. When these cards appear in a layout for reading, they represent the most important things that the questioner (in Tarot readings, called the 'querent') wants to learn. Some of the images on the cards are self evident; others are fanciful, such as the House of God, depicted as a tower struck by lightning with two people being hurled to the ground.

The Minor Arcana, or Lesser Secrets, is made up

of fifty-six cards. They are divided into four suits: cups, batons, swords and coins. They are numbered, as with regular playing cards, and have four court cards, the page, knight, queen and king. The numbered cards represent everyday situations, the court cards the various people who might affect the questioner's life.

When the cards are used in a reading, each one has a different meaning. When placed upright, generally positive, when reversed (meaning upside-down), generally negative.

# THE MAJOR ARCANA

## I * THE MAGICIAN

When upright, key words for the Magician are dexterity and

flexibility, information and communication. The latter attribute relates this card to the Egyptian god, Thoth, who was thought to have created heiroglyphics. Reversed, the card can suggest confusion, lack of inspiration, slyness or indecision.

# II * THE HIGH PRIESTESS

Also known as the Female Pope, the High Priestess is the feminine principle. She is a symbol of virginity, through the Virgin Mary, and mysticism, through her identification with the Egyptian goddess, Isis. Many cards identify her with Pope Joan in 858 ad, whose deception was discovered when she gave birth on the steps of St Peter's in Rome.

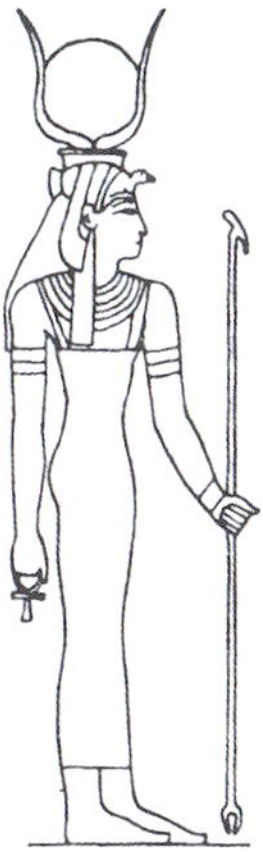

Upright, she represents intuition and premonition, reproduction and observation.

Reversed, she can suggest repression and ignorance, sexual manipulation and fantasies.

# III * THE EMPRESS

The Empress is a symbol of feminine power, related to mother-goddesses, rather than imperious royalty. She can be both bride and mother, and is identified with Demeter (Ceres), representing the fertility of the earth. The eagle on her shield shows her earthly powers. Dealt upright, she shows abundance and reproduction, compassion and companionship. Reversed, she suggests dependency and timidity, fear of affection and difficulties in sustaining relationships.

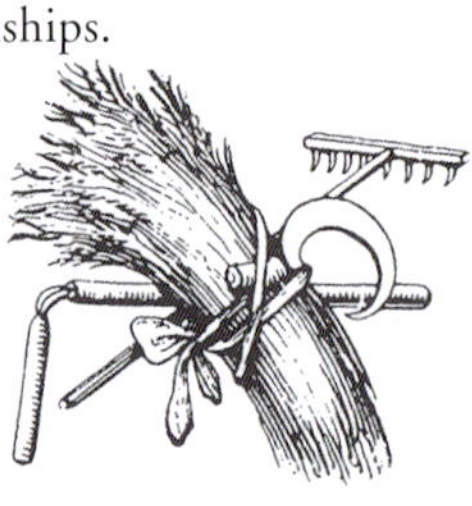

# IV * THE EMPEROR

The Emperor is the symbol of masculine power, related to the great heroes of antiquity. They need not be warrior-kings, but mythological father-gods such as Thor, and gods of great creative energy. Upright, the Emperor breathes self-assertion, motivation, and vigour. Reversed, he may show intolerance and aggression, impatience and immaturity. This card can predict ruthlessness and ambition.

# V * THE POPE

Also known as the Hierophant (from the Greek for 'one who explains'), the Pope balances the Emperor's temporal power. He is the other side of the High Priestess, or Female Pope, representing analytical rather than intuitive intelligence. He is the spirit

of education, temporal and spiritual; he is closely related to the Egyptian god, Osiris, and the Greek god, Zeus, shown opposite. Wise teaching and revelations, fraternity and marriage, when upright, can be countered by dogmatism and orthodoxy when reversed.

# VI * THE LOVERS

The key element of this card is choice; choice between people, choice between the spiritual or sensual or, more mundanely, a choice between prospective employers. But ultimately, whatever the choice, commitment will prevail. Cupid hovers menacingly over the lovers, ready to shoot the arrow of irrationality, while the elder person advises caution. Displayed upright, the Lovers bring emotional security and harmony, togetherness and faithfulness. Reversed, they take you into the realms of promiscuity and obsession, infidelity and deception.

# VII * THE CHARIOT

The Chariot carries an occupant who has been so triumphant in his quest that he does not need to hold the reins. His victory has been spiritual, as well as material. It

is the war-chariot of Mars or the Indian juggernaut, carrying a warning not to crush anything, or anyone, lying in your path. Even its positive aspects can suggest confrontation, though it also represents well-deserved victory through knowledge of what can be achieved. Reversed, it can lead to envy and avarice, over-ambition and distraction.

# VIII * JUSTICE

This is one of the simpler cards to understand as it is a visual representation of the need to be logical, to balance arguments and being diplomatic. It can also mean balance in Nature, the ecological approach. The opposites of these attributes apply when reversed. This card is identified with the Greek goddess of justice.

# IX * THE HERMIT

The sage of legend lights the way ahead on the path to self-enlightenment. He leads to inner calm and discretion, meditation and reassessment. He represents the wisdom that time brings and introduces us to helpful aides.

Reversed, it can show introversion and alienation, obstinacy and immaturity. Genuine offers of help may be foolishly spurned.

# X * THE WHEEL OF FORTUNE

The Wheel of Fortune does not necessarily revolve relentlessly. In positive aspect, it is the path of the sun across the heavens. It suggests acceptance, rather than resignation, and that opportunities often present themselves in disguise. It shows the power of coincidence in life and can herald positive upheaval. The drama of losing a job may propel you into a better one. The card's negative aspects suggest difficulties and delays, rather than full-stops. It can also suggest that current problems could make unwelcome reappearances.

# XI * STRENGTH

As well as physical strength, this card signifies moral courage, optimism and good resolve. Some cards portray Hercules killing the lion, whose skin will give him invincibility. Others show a nymph fearlessly opening the lion's mouth, as though she had some magic hold over it. Reversed, it can demonstrate vanity and pomposity, unbridled sensuality and lust.

# XII * THE HANGED MAN

This is not a card of evil meaning, in spite of the image. It simply suggests some sacrifice due, a period of delay, a transformation and rebirth, a recurring theme in most mythologies. Although these attributes seem negative,

they are not as negative as when the card is reversed, indicating selfishness and resignation, victimization and self-absorption.

In Norse mythology, Odin hung himself on the World Tree to attain great knowledge.

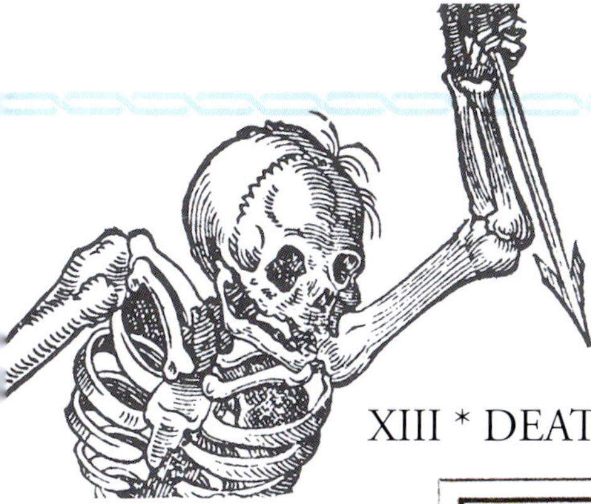

# XIII * DEATH

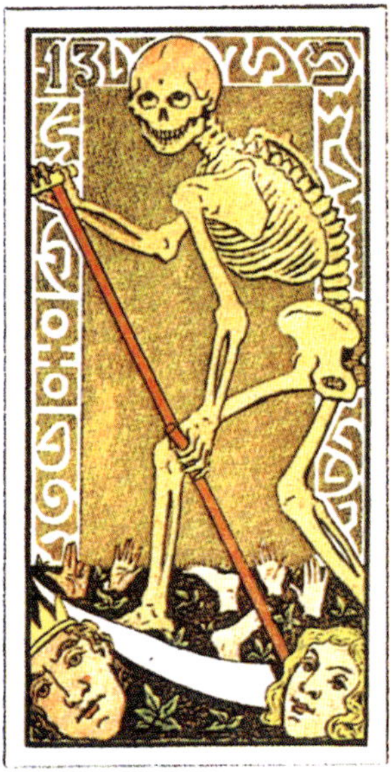


Death is the only democracy and is therefore a warning to both great and humble, as the image on the card shows. It can mean change through sacrifice, renewal following loss, or a passage through an ordeal to rebirth. Reversed, it presages physical or mental exhaustion, impotency or inactivity.

# XIV * TEMPERANCE

A simple image of a simple concept, embodying time as a healer, balance and harmony, enlightenment and moderation. Even the negative aspects are mild; a too delicate nature, physical stress, or restlessness, arising from its affinity to the Moon goddess.

# XV * THE DEVIL

This card is the most negative in The Tarot, but if the challenge is taken head on, the adversary can be beaten. It poses questions about our own negativity, suggesting that a more positive line should be taken. Financial gain can be heralded, but beware. You may not enjoy the benefits of it. It suggests a time for prudence and self-questioning. Its many negative meanings include the Seven Deadly Sins.

# XVI * THE TOWER

Major changes are presaged by this card, the lightning coming from God as portrayed in the Old Testament or from Zeus, as in Greek mythology. The Tower can act as a cleanser, causing disruption, anger and agitation, but leading to enlightenment. If the positive attributes seem severe, the negative are more so, ranging from vandalism to misogyny and oppression.

# XVII * THE STAR

Following the destruction of the Tower, comes the new beginning of the Star. Hope, or Aphrodite, whose morning star heralds a new dawn, pours the waters of life onto the land to revive it. It brings a new stream of knowledge and inspiration, causing mental renewal. When reversed, pessimism and self-doubt can lead to time-wasting and a lack of concern for fellow human beings.

# XVIII * THE MOON

The world of the unconscious, the world of dreams and nightmares. Its association with night makes it the card of the shadowy side of human feelings. The dogs on the card reflect a connection with Anubis, the jackal-headed god of the Egyptian afterlife. The water represents the primeval soup from which human beings emerged. It is a card of mothering, nurturing and sacrifice. When reversed, it is a card of trickery, insincerity and vulnerability.

# XIX * THE SUN

The sun's rays can blind, as well as illuminate, the latter attribute shining strongly in The Tarot. It is the card of good fortune in life; health, wealth and happiness. It brings vitality and confidence. If it is reversed, or crosses another favourable card, it can introduce doubt, delay happiness, or blind you, so that you cannot see what the true situation is. To the ancient Egyptians the sun was the principal god and for the ancient Greeks he was Apollo, god of the arts and healing.

# XX * JUDGMENT

Portraying the Last Day of Judgment, this card reveals that what you do in life will be judged, not only in heaven, but by those around you. Judged harshly, relationships can be broken and employment problematic. Judge as you wish to be judged. Connected with the concept of rebirth,

Judgment can indicate a good time to change work or home, even country. It makes separation from a loved one, or favourite object, only temporary. Negatively, it brings phobias and obsessions, stagnation and guilt.

# XXI * THE WORLD

The last numbered card of The Tarot represents completion and fulfilment. The naked woman dances in a wreath, or halo, with a symbol at each corner. The symbols are the creatures belonging to the four fixed signs of the Zodiac – Aquarius, Scorpio, Taurus and Leo. The World represents the end of a cycle, a chapter of life. Positively, it marks accomplishment, a recognition of achievement and worldly success. Reversed, it can bring delay and frustration, martyrdom for a cause or worldly worries.

♌ Leo

♏ Scorpius

♒ Aquarius

# THE FOOL

The Fool appears at the end of the journey through The Tarot and is ready for new beginnings. His knapsack represents his worldly goods, his staff, his willpower.

Often he is accompanied by a dog snapping at his heels, representing the world of instinct. In some ways he is Fate, always present and oft-times capricious. His mocking laughter can be heard in the distance when portentous decisions are made. He is the agent of elusive luck, which can turn at any moment.

Beware his appearance in a reading. He is a challenge to tread warily.

# PREPARATION FOR READING

Beginners should choose an uncomplicated pack, such as the Rider Waite or Swiss, with crystal-clear images. There are many modern packs, with different themes, which are excellent works of art, but can introduce confusing elements. However, you may find one to suit you; compatibility is the key word. A pack with an illustrated Minor Arcana will make life easier; memorizing their meanings from numbers alone is tiring and may make reading laboured.

A reading should not be approached casually, like a game of cards. Make a ritual out of it. Create an atmosphere of trust. Light a scented candle, or use a little incense. Shuffle the cards gently and deal deliberately, face down, into the arrangement for the chosen reading. Then turn uniformly, as though turning the pages of a book.

# THE CELTIC CROSS

This reading is extremely helpful for both particular or general queries. It can predict or advise. Its only limit is that it is better for another's life, than your own. As numbered opposite, the first card gives an idea of the present situation, the second, an impediment or encouragement, depending on the card. The third card starts you on the road to a solution. Card four looks over the distant past, the fifth, the recent past. Card six opens the path to future actions and to the possible solutions offered by the last four cards. They, respectively, take the first step away from present difficulties, give encouragement and introduce a 'rogue' element. The last card completes the cross and offers a solution.

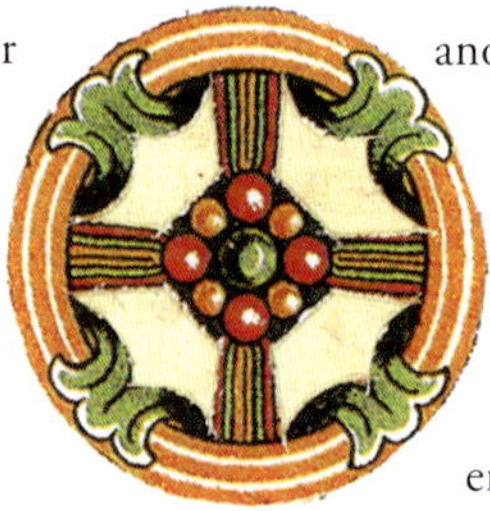

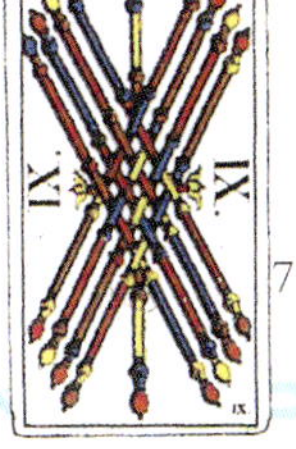


Using only the cards from the Major Arcana can provide clearer, if simpler, guidance when dealing with major issues.

# THE MINOR ARCANA

Having mastered the Major Arcana and how to use it, divination by Tarot can be refined by the inclusion of the Minor Arcana. Key words and attributes of the cards must be learned. Upright cards reflect the positive influence; reversed, the negative. The court cards, with their different characteristics, are particularly important.

## CUPS (*chalices, hearts*)

ACE: loving domesticity; a feeling of emptiness

TWO: fortune and how to secure it; set on a treadmill

THREE: reunions and relationships; impetuosity in business

FOUR: new friendships; marital prospects disturbed

FIVE: too dependent; indecision through jealousy

SIX: affinity and socializing; beware of impositions

SEVEN: be realistic; beware fickle friends

EIGHT: reflect and understand; superficial friendships

NINE: dreams can come true; excessive indulgence

TEN: consolidation of family; instability

Page (*knave or jack*); renewed contacts; introversion

Knight: a chance to be be grasped now; impressionable

Queen: a faithful woman; insensitivity

King: a well-intentioned man; can mislead

## BATONS (*wands, clubs*)

ACE: success and lifelong friendship; energy deficiency

TWO: make ideas reality; opposition from close associates

THREE: set an example; a break-up, divorce and remarriage

FOUR: mutual help; financial loss caused by false friends

FIVE: a profitable marriage; facing blank walls

SIX: profitable business partnership; tendency to pretence

SEVEN: confront obstacles; beware the opposite sex

EIGHT: new ideas and challenges; someone may expropriate money

NINE: accept offers of help; a feud with friends

Ten: bear heavy responsibilities; the loss of a close one

Page: keep an open mind; don't over-exert yourself

Knight: support from unfamiliar source; over-imposition

Queen: make things happen; overbearing

King: an inspirational man; domineering

## SWORDS (*spades*)

ACE: determination; misfortune and news of death

TWO: balance and reflection; serious loss and separation

THREE: communicate your troubles; misfortune in love

FOUR: pace yourself; ill-health causing delays

FIVE: success, but only after overcoming obstacles; rejection

SIX: perseverance needed to complete objectives; slow thinking

SEVEN: vigilance; broken friendships cause troubles

EIGHT: be patient; caution when dealing with shallow friends

NINE: explain your troubles; sickness and related unhappiness

Ten: get it out of your system;
grief and negative aspects

Page: don't rush to conclusions;
beware envious people

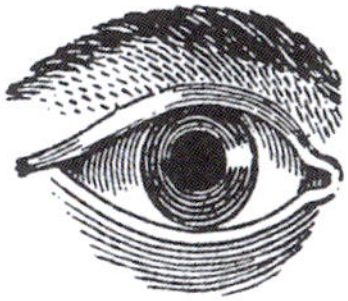

Knight: take the challenge;
restrain extravagance

Queen: be careful;
treachery is in the air

King: delegate power;
restrain over-
reaching ambition

## COINS (*pentacles, diamonds*)

ACE: an important message is due; out of touch

TWO: become adaptable; stubborn and fixed mind

THREE: be practical; a sign of impending quarrels

FOUR: look after your future; friends may betray you

FIVE: take care of yourself; financial problems ahead

SIX: be aware of your worth; lack of prudence with resources

SEVEN: success through perseverance; rumours circulate

EIGHT: work at it; travel may distract

NINE: recognition imminent; tendency to assume it already

TEN: money, money, money; selfishness in financial matters

PAGE: change of job or home; unwelcome news around the corner

KNIGHT; persevere to make a discovery; not see the new idea

QUEEN: be creative; confuse the creative ideas

KING: efforts pay off; obstinate and obsessed.

# THE HORSESHOE SPREAD

This reading shows a mixture of cards from the Minor and Major Arcana. It is a good reading for direct answers to direct questions. In the example opposite, the Three of Cups reversed suggests a sensible move (if upright it would have indicated hasty decisions). The Seven of Swords suggests conflict, an argument possibly. The third card, the reversed Emperor, indicates some formal resolution of that problem, but it will be pointless. The reversed Wheel of Fortune means holding back and not taking hasty actions. The Six of Batons advises that the quarrel may subside, whilst Temperance enforces this view. The outcome is shown by the reversed Queen of Cups; a specific reference to a troublesome woman.

This could be read as person A falling out with a friend, B, after provocation from a woman, C.

Matters could reach court, but A plays cool, counting on the strength of old friendship. The argument blows over, A and B become friends again. C's provocation has been has proved fruitless.

# TAROT AND YOUR HEALTH

The cards of the Major Arcana can indicate impending problems.

## The Magician

Expect some stress, with difficulties in finding the source of the problem.

## The High Priestess

Whatever the physical problem you can expect a fast recovery.

## The Empress

The onset of back problems, alleviated by a restful holiday.

## The Emperor

Sexual problems, mental or physical, are at the point of being resolved.

## The Pope

Respiratory troubles could be the problem, with short breath and possible chest pains.

## The Lovers

You will be sexually active and your physical state will constantly improve.

## The Chariot

Anxiety will result if you do not take things at an easier pace. Slow down!

## Justice

Possible dental problems have been building up.

## The Hermit

A physical check-up is called for, but all will be well.

## The Wheel of Fortune

Problems of over-indulgence of food and emotional ups and downs.

## Strength

Dynamic energy is indicated; enough to overcome any impending handicap.

## The Hanged Man

Take a break and avoid people who exhaust your energy.

## Death

Talking about life and death will change your attitude to life.

## Temperance

An old problem will return, but only a mild one.

## The Devil

Sleeping problems brought on by being a workaholic.

## The Tower

An accident may bring unforeseen medical expenses.

## The Star

Medical tests may be on the horizon. Take care!

## The Moon

Your body tells you of impending problems, with possible sleep problems.

## The Sun

Things are not as good as they should be, with feelings of inertia.

## Judgment

More anxiety, but in the work-place, or through legal problems.

## The World

Take time recuperating from over-strain or illness.

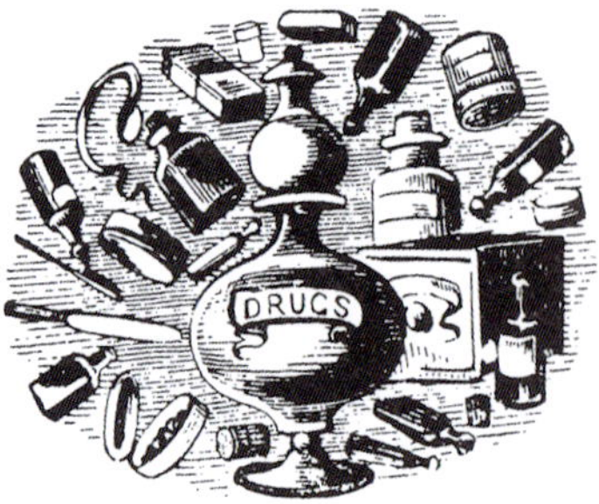


## The Fool

Don't delay in seeking medical help if you are feeling down.

# TAROT AND RELATIONSHIPS

Compatibility is paramount when establishing firm relationships. The Major Arcana can provide useful pointers in that direction.

The Magician conjures up a new relationship, while the High Priestess suggests you don't want or need one.

Longing for deep affection is brought by the Empress and Lovers are brought together by the Emperor. The Pope offers either intense love, or no love at all, while the Lovers can mean partings. The Chariot brings speedy affairs; Justice few, but true, partnerships. From the Hermit's cave, an old flame may emerge, which is also suggested by the Wheel of Fortune. But you are in two minds about meeting. Strength you do not have, when this card appears. You are not ready to make a commitment. . .

. . . The Hanged Man is, literally, in suspense, waiting to see what a partner may do and the Devil tells that, though your love continues, a relationship may end. A lover from your past is indicated by Temperance, but what are your feelings? It could be someone you still have hopes for,

especially if the Devil turns up. Like the Tower, your plans will crumble through emotional deception. A lack of love in your relationship is reinforced by the Star; if you try to make things work, it warns of disillusionment. The Sun at least brings hope that someone out there is desperately wishing to gain your affections. Judgment, unfairly, makes you doubt someone's sincerity, particularly when restarting an old relationship. As the World must constantly revolve, new beginnings can be looked forward to.

## PRAISE OF VENUS

Yea all these things well praised may be
But with what words shall we praise thee
O VENUS O thou love alive
Born to give peace to souls that strive

# TAROT AND PERSONAL FINANCE

Great experience is needed to apply the wisdom of The Tarot to the intricacies of today's financial world.

In general, the Magician promises business success. The High Priestess counsels patience building up that success. Dealt together they tell you not to rush into business deals. The Empress suggests delay in payment, the Emperor unblocking the hold-up. The Pope also suggests irritating delays; a cheque lost in the post, or a computer muddle. The Lovers promise consistent finance through your own skills, but you may have to fight for payment if they are coupled with the Chariot. Justice suggests

shortage of funds, but when the Hermit appears, so does extra money. The Wheel of Fortune tells of dwindling reserves, but Strength assures that funds will be found. Beware the excessive demands of the Hanged Man, which, linked to Death, will presage financial failure. But Temperance offers a helping hand. The Devil's run on your money will not prove catastrophic. But the Tower will be! Watch out for medical expenses. Hope to cross it with the Star, which promises rosy prospects. Under the Moon, debts will be repaid, but not in full. For that, the Sun must shine or Judgment reign. The World offers hope of unexpected funds. A tax rebate?

ACKNOWLEDGMENTS

Cards from the Pierpoint-Morgan Visconti Tarocchi pack reproduced by permission of U.S. Games Systems, Inc. Illustrations are from the Tate Gallery and the British Museum, London, the Russell Cotes Art Gallery, Bournemouth, the Corcoran Collection and Grapharchive.

The publishers have made every effort to identify all illustration sources. Any errors and omissions will be corrected in future editions.